Sabbath Time

*a hermitage journey of
retreat, return & communion*

Charles R. Ringma
Illustrated by Teresa Jordan

Copyright©Charles Ringma

The moral rights of Charles Ringma to be identified as the Author of this Work has been asserted in accordance with the Copyright, Designs and Patent Act 1988

This edition published by Piquant Editions in 2017
Piquant Editions is an imprint of Piquant.
Piquant
PO Box 83, Carlisle, CA3 9GR, UK

ISBNs:
978-1-909281-57-8
Charles Ringma: Sabbath Time - OD
978-1-909281-58-5
Charles Ringma: Sabbath Time - Mobi

All rights reserved. No part of this publication may be reproduced, stored in a retrieval system, or transmitted in any form or by any means, electronic, mechanical, photocopying, recording, or otherwise, without the prior permission of both the copyright owner and the publisher of the book.

British Library Cataloguing in Publication Data
A catalogue record for this book is available from the British Library
ISBN 978-1-909281-57-8

Cover design and Typesetting by ProjectLuz.com

For

Terry and Rosie Gatfield

*whose hermitage set in the Queensland bush
was a haven of tranquility*

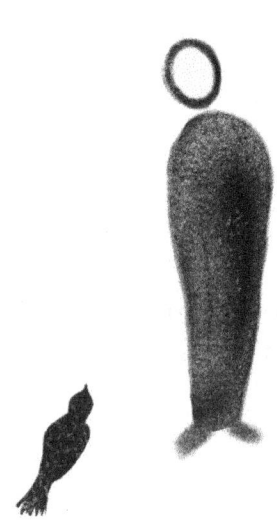

Contents

Into the Hermitage

Downtime	2
Wandering	4
Being	6
Gazing	8
Waiting	10
Reading	12
Indwelling	14
Attentiveness	16
Crying Out	18
Seeing	20
Seeing Anew	22
Sabbath Space	24
Troubling God	26
Responding	28
Repentance	30
Hidden Water	32
Memory and Hope	34
Encountering	36
For the Life of the World	38
A Long Journey	40

The Journey Home

The Call to Return	44
Returning as a Pilgrim	46
Returning as Stranger	48
Returning with Glory	50

Communion

Disorientation	54
Imagination	56
Connection	58
This Day	60

Preface

Like many of my Christian friends I have gone on retreats from time to time. And in some of the places where I have worked, an annual retreat was part of the ethos of the place. Usually, these retreats were over a one-week period. Apart from a few occasions, I usually took some other work with me. Teaching always called for the development of a new course, student papers to grade, academic advising, and the new book to write.

Thus while I sought to be attentive to the purpose of the retreat, I usually managed to cram in other work. I guess that says a lot about me and the way I operate. Simply put, I drank in the Protestant work ethic along with my mother's milk—and I tend to overwork.

A serious health breakdown in my thirties, where I spent over six months in recovery, made me aware of the need for greater balance in my life. Yet since then, I have continued to do too much, say "yes" instead of "no" too often, and I have struggled to set aside time for rest, prayer, and reflection. I think this will remain an ongoing struggle for me till the very end.

But finally, after a year of thought and planning, I decided to take a whole six months off and to spend much of this time in a hermitage on friends' property. I am grateful to them for the gift of this place and grateful to my family and friends, with whom I am involved in many activities, for the gift of space. Being left alone to embark on a reflective journey is a great gift—particularly in our age, where remaining connected is such a driving expectation.

To enter a space of disconnection is both a scary and an exhilarating experience. And to "down" tools and be still without an agenda of expectations is wonderfully open and freeing. It is also walking into mystery. Who knows what might happen?

I did not set out to write anything in the hermitage, let alone have something published. But from time to time, I wrote some reflections, and in the skilful editing hands of Karen Hollenbeck-Wuest, these now appear as this book. Thank you, Karen! And a big thank you to Pieter Kwant, my literary agent, who always manages to persuade some publisher to put writings such as these into print. And finally my joy that Teresa Jordan's art has given this book a haunting and evocative atmosphere.

Charles Ringma,
Brisbane, Australia, 2017

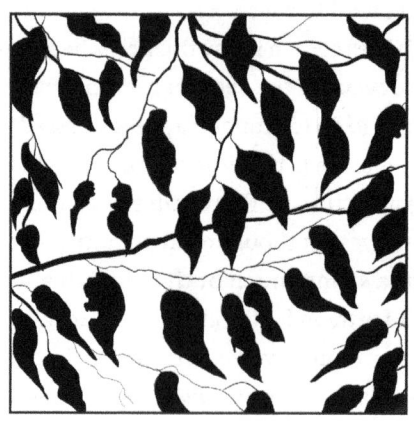

Introduction

To some extent this book needs no introduction. These reflections should speak for themselves. Yet this whole book may seem irrelevant because I am writing about *my* retreat time. Since we all bring our own biography, reasons, and hopes to any enterprise, what is a helpful time for some may not be so for others.

However, Henri Nouwen's oft-repeated remark—that what is most personal may also be most universal—is worth considering. This is especially true within a Christian framework that is characterized by commonalities: a common Scripture, a common faith in Christ, a common Spirit, a common calling to be with God in prayer and meditation, and a common calling to serve the world. This fundamental commonality shaped by the gospel and the presence of Christ in each of our lives gives us a common identity and set of values despite all our cultural, ethnic, and gender differences.

Moreover, we all need down-time. We all need to participate in the fundamental rhythm of engagement and disengagement. We are all called to be more prayerful. We all need to set aside time to reflect.

More significantly, we are all characterised by longing and hope. And we all need to find space so that our truer selves can break through the constructs of our social selves so that our performance-based orientation to life can be undermined by the joy of a self well-loved in the grace of God.

While I do not wish to dwell on the dualities of being and doing, contemplation and action, prayer and service, it is rather obvious that in this pragmatic age, our default mode is towards activism—especially since prayer has become somewhat superfluous in the Christian community due to a growing sense that God has left us to our own devices.

The invitation to a Sabbath spirituality is designed not simply to renew our energies so that we are "bright and chirpy" for work on Monday morning and the rest of the week, but rather to renew us in the love of God. Such a spirituality can sustain us, help us to resist the powers of our age, and empower us for creative engagement with our world. But this spirituality needs the gift of time. One may not be able to give it six months or even a week's retreat, but it needs to become integral to our lives of worship, faith, and service. Thus we need to cultivate a Sabbath spirituality in our lives, no matter how busy our schedules.

This small set of reflections is not a challenge to "do the same," nor a formulaic recipe for Sabbath spirituality. It is simply a witness, and the challenge is to do something in this direction that works for you.

Into the Hermitage

1

Downtime

6 May 2016

Since the first of April, I have "downed" tools, so to speak, for a six-month sabbatical. But this is not the usual kind of academic sabbatical, where the idea is to work really hard on researching or producing my next book. Instead, I am trying to be as unproductive as possible. During this downtime, I will be still, reflective, and let my life lie fallow. As a consequence, I have pulled out of all my usual activities.

    You might ask what has brought this on? Health issues? Overwork? A faith crisis? Actually, none of these things! And no clear inner voice has spoken to me, let alone a voice from heaven. I simply had a growing sense over the past year that just as the land needs to lie fallow, so perhaps from time to time one's life needs to as well. I thought that I would put this simple notion into practice and see what this could be like.

One of the major challenges in freeing up my time has been getting family, friends, and colleagues to agree so that I could pull out of my usual commitments. Generally, this process has gone reasonably well. But it has not been easy to explain this time to others—in large part because I have never walked (crawled) this road before. Also, I am not at all clear what to expect.

Another challenge has been dealing with my internal motivations regarding this downtime. Being somewhat compulsive and hard-working, a key question has been—and continues to be—am I doing this for a particular outcome? New spiritual insights? Renewal? A new book? I am still wrestling with this. To be—rather than to achieve a particular outcome - which is the sacred mantra of our present age - is a constant challenge.

This first month has been pretty messy! Quite a number of things have come my way that needed immediate attention. So my first lesson: there is no clean start to this downtime journey, and the life around me will continue to impact me, whether or not I am on retreat. Not that I wanted to escape from life's realities—as this is never possible, since we are part of the fabric of life. And not even monastics are beyond the blessings and madness of our world.

But the rhythm of my day is more or less monastic. At various times during the day I stop to be, reflect, pray, and read scripture. And each afternoon, I spend time at a hermitage that a good friend built on his property "for God." There I am in the Aussie bush, with gentle breezes, the songs of birds, and the visit of the occasional wallaby. I am happy to be in this God-space.

2

Wandering

10 May 2016

Since the global financial crisis, we have all become familiar with the term "free fall." The idea is that large parts of the global economy are in free fall, spinning out of control with a momentum all their own—and no one knows when or where it will end.

The contemplative experience can also feel like we are in free fall as we suspend ourselves from the ordinary structures and the usual busyness of life. Instead of completing a task and moving on to the next one—and living with both the satisfaction or frustration of this—we enter a vast open space. Our initial sense may be that we can wander uninterrupted through this uncluttered terrain. How freeing this is!

But this is most often a mirage. For a vast open space often causes anxiety. We seem to be happier with tasks, demands, projects, structures. While we clamour for freedom, we don't quite know what to do with it.

So it is for me. In this vast open space, I am barraged not with quietness, but with a phalanx of questions that march towards me. *Where is the decisive redemptive and healing action of God in our broken world? Why does our all-pervasive culture, which seems to be incapable of sustaining a life of goodness, continue to be so influential? Why does conflict continue to be so much a part of our world? Why do the causes for justice continue to be thwarted? Why does the church continue to be such a fragile and marginal institution? Does a life of prayer really matter? How can I more truly live the gospel? What of the brokenness of my own life?*

The unerring questions march on. I hear them. I taste them. I feel them. They invade this space and unsettle me. For there are no real answers.

The contemplative journey is neither a sure-footed stroll nor a walk along a rocky road. It is more like losing one's way in an unfamiliar landscape. There is no road through this vast terrain. While it may be empty, I am not. And because I am not, the terrain is not. The marchers keep coming towards me, and sometimes I feel that I am in free fall. Nothing secure is under my feet.

Though I do not revel in this state, I do not want to be rescued. Instead, I will seek to remain here as long as necessary. I have no sense of what this time may yield. In this way, it is a journey of faith.

<u>3</u>

Being

15 May 2016

We speak a lot these days about human agency. This concept proclaims that we can *do* something and that we can and should act even in the face of overwhelming odds. While we all act into the world in a whole variety of ways, it is all too obvious that some people make a much greater impact (for good or ill) than others.

This also means that some people may feel that they have little influence. And this may well lead to various forms of passive resignation. This may well become the pervasive sense that many people have in the face of the powers—the powerful institutions of our time amidst the merger of political, banking, multinational, and military configurations.

Anyone who is part of any protest movement today is aware of the entrenchment of power and the questionable effect we have in advocating another way.

Yet it is important that we continue to act into life, even when we know that we can do little. Scholars have rightly emphasized that we are most fundamentally creatures of externalization. We say and do things. We dream and make things. We shape our lives, relationships, and world in some way. We are actors, if you like, in the human arena.

This idea has theological resonance. Created in the image of God, we are called by this Creator God to shape the human community. However, this shaping is to reflect the redemptive and healing passion of God and the quest for justice and the common good.

What happens when a person "downs" tools and enters a time of non-engagement, Sabbath spirituality, reflection, and prayer? And what if this downtime is for an extended period—not just an hour in a day, but a time of days, weeks, or even months?

There are no simple and singular answers to these questions. But there are some key contours. The most obvious is that it is difficult to "down" tools. And quickly following on the heels of this, it is easy to feel useless, even if we are spending more time in meditation and prayer. But more deeply and corrosively, we can become more anxious and fearful. It is as if everything on our horizon looms larger and darker.

A possible implication of this is that *not* acting increases our levels of anxiety and powerlessness. Thus human agency is psychologically beneficial. To act and to do something staves off the sense of chaos that can overwhelm us.

This raises a question about the value of Sabbath time. What about taking time out from our busy activities? What about taking time to reflect and to pray? Is that not doing something? Is that not exercising human agency? Is that not also acting into life, but in a very different way?

It is, but this different way leads us into very unfamiliar territory. It is the road less travelled. And while this road may lead to certain outcomes, more likely it will be shrouded in mystery. And while it may lead to peace, we will need to confront demons, and a certain denuding will need to take place, particularly the stripping away of the illusions of our work-a-day world and the ideas that our busyness is helpful and productive.

The challenge here is clear enough. We need to find the way of prayer as another path of human agency. And this will undoubtedly call for a profound reorientation, since prayer is often seen as a useless waste of time or a cop-out. In the challenging days ahead, this path may become for me the way towards a more authentic way of being.

<u>4</u>

Gazing

29 May 2016

Sitting on the verandah of the hermitage each afternoon, I look straight down an incline to a large earthenware bowl full of water, where all sorts of birds come to drink, ringing their melodies through the bushland. The most melodious is the small Lewin's Honeyeater. The most raucous is the Noisy Friarbird, who thinks the hermitage was built for it. But the most stately is the repeated call of the Pied Currawong, particularly as the afternoon sun wanes and shadows creep through the trees. And then there are the occasional visits of a Swamp Wallaby, who drinks so much that it seems to be tanking up at a petrol station.

My gaze past the earthenware bowl falls on a double cross made of rough wood. The small cross attached to a larger cross suggests that we are the beneficiaries of the death of Christ on the cross, but we also enter into and share his suffering as we carry our own cross.

Past the wooden cross, my gaze is drawn down the valley, up a distant mountain, then to the sky above. To my right, a single tree with three powerful trunks reaches for the sky. I call it the Trinitarian tree.

Apart from the bird calls and the breeze, the Aussie bush is wrapped in silence. This silence is invitational. Over time, the outerscape becomes part of my innerscape, my soulscape. When the wind blows from the southeast, I can sometimes hear the muted hum of traffic, but when the wind blows from the northwest, a total silence envelops me. Occasionally an aircraft high in the sky heading either southwest or northwest intrudes into my brooding or joyful silence.

Yesterday I spent ages watching the dance of brightly coloured butterflies. The butterfly never flies in a straight line, but dances all over the place. Every so often, two or more butterflies dance in harmony, but never for very long. Watching these delightful creatures of the "light fantastic" makes me wonder about my movement through life. So much is about planning, strategizing, progressing, achieving. We move from point "a" to get to point "b," and we expect a straight line. But perhaps life is more about the surprise, the unexpected, the sudden open door? Maybe it is more like the dance of butterflies?

In case you are curious, I am not using any meditational strategies. I am familiar with contemporary writers on centering and contemplative prayer, and Thomas Merton has long been my companion in reflection. But at present I am more interested in gazing and being quiet.

I am aware that in my previous reflection I left open the question of a crisis of prayer in our modern world. I will come back to this sometime. But at present I am with the butterflies.

5

Waiting

3 June 2016

In our culture, we tend to expect things to happen quickly if not instantaneously. Our current communication technology has certainly fostered this expectation, which has filtered into our religiosity. Many expect God to be at their beck and call and are puzzled when the supposed Almighty God appears to be so slow.

The current interest in contemplative practices amongst some Christians needs careful reflection lest this practice becomes steeped in a quick-fix set of expectations. One way to gain a clarity is to distinguish between contemplative practices and the gift of contemplation. To put that in somewhat different and possibly more Barthian language, contemplation is both a task and a gift.

The task part is well known and receives much attention in contemporary literature. Most of us are familiar with the small steps we can take in the cultivating of the art of contemplation: finding a quiet place, learning to be still, attending to our breathing, using a Jesus Prayer or a mantra, laying things down, being attentive to the Spirit's inner working, reflecting on a key word of Scripture. But in this we must remember that contemplation is an art and not a set of techniques.

Practicing contemplation on a regular basis can certainly form our spirituality and foster our health and well-being. It can also shape us to become more reflective and less driven, which can deepen our relationship with God. As we tend the art of contemplation, it becomes a part of our very being rather than our modus operandi. Over time, these practices become easier and more doable as we carry them with us into other relationships and the workplace. All of this is good and augurs a better world.

But the gift of contemplation is the vision of God or some other transcendent experience of the divine, which is given at God's behest—and not as a result of our prowess or our activities. The task is what we can do. The gift is God's prerogative.

It is good that this is so, for we live in a world of processes and outcomes. Instrumentality is our big game. We do *this* in order to gain *that*. Our relationship with God can so easily become technologized. To put that in stronger language, our game is often to manipulate God for our own ends.

While contemplative practices are helpful, our longing should be for the gift that God alone can give. Such a gift of the vision of God can forever enlighten and change us. We need this gift in order to see through the facades of our world into the heart of God. In this way, our eyes are opened with wonder and purpose.

In the midst of these contemplative practices, I wait for God's gift.

6

Reading

26 June 2016

In this time away from more normal duties and responsibilities, I not only spend time at the hermitage, but I am also seeking to bring the hermitage home, as it were, into my daily life. Each day I read Scripture, though I am neither reading the Bible in a scholarly way nor in the discipline of *lectio divina*.

I read from the Pentateuch, the Wisdom literature, the prophets, the Gospels and from the Pauline letters. And to help me remain attentive, I read in English, Dutch, German, and in New Testament Greek. Sadly, my four years of Old Testament Hebrew have long ago faded into oblivion. My loss, no doubt!

My approach to this reading is not systematic, but rather random and leisurely. I seek to be attentive to what I am reading, but I have no immediate purpose in mind. I am not reading in order to produce a lecture, a homily, or anything else for that matter.

Some things have struck me, and none have been revolutionary. I also have no sense that God has spoken specifically to me through Scripture, but only generally in terms of the scope of the biblical story. This is okay. I am not trying to make something special happen. Here is what has stood out for me:

First, the biblical story is strange and comes from such another world.

Second, so much of the Bible, especially the Old Testament, is harsh and unacceptable to modern sensibilities, particularly punishments with their emphasis on violence.

Third, since that ancient world is shrouded in mystery, there is much that does not readily make sense.

Fourth, despite this and other matters of concern, the biblical narrative is clear about God's engagement with his people and his involvement in human affairs. This, too, is strange, for in our contemporary secular world, God seems to be absent.

Fifth, the overriding sense one gains from the biblical story is that God is the Creator, a Seeking God who offers us restoration and healing. What immediately follows from this is that God's desire and purpose is for us to live life in the ambit and joy and task of cooperating with God's renewing work in the world.

Sixth, I would venture to say that the Bible makes little sense unless, like St. Paul, one has received a revelation of Christ and is seeking to live in the way of Christ through the inspiration of the Spirit. After all, the Old Testament prophets point to Christ; the Gospels display the life of Christ; and the epistles map out the implications of what it means to live in, with, and for Christ in the faith community and the world. While the written Word may lead us towards the living Word, Jesus Christ, the living Word certainly helps us attend to the written Word.

Seventh, there are frameworks that help us make general sense of the biblical story. One is the three-fold movement of creation, fall, and restoration. Another is the concept of covenant that God makes with his Old Testament people and then with those who are in Christ Jesus. These and other frameworks, including reading Scripture eschatologically, are helpful.

But there are two other important frameworks. One is to read Scripture in terms of its liberating impulses and to favour these when they seem to clash with themes that reflect the culture of the time when Scripture was written. Secondly, Scripture can be read dialectically. These themes are writ everywhere in the biblical story: God beyond nature and God in nature, God's sovereignty and human responsibility, the Exodus and the Captivity, Jesus as God and Jesus as Man, the Christian as sinner and saint, all things new in God's final future and the continuation of the old. The dialectic framework saves us from mono-themes that so easily pervert the richness of God's truth.

This probably does not make reading Scripture any more attractive, but it helps me engage the biblical narratives. I do know that this book can shape our lives and give us a different way of being in our culture. And maybe that is what it seeks to do.

7

Indwelling

29 June 2016

I am aware that the time will soon come when I will return to the normal routines of life, and this extended season in the hermitage will come to an end and begin to fade.

I need to be clear that this Sabbath time does not reflect some deeper piety or hold some virtue in and of itself. We don't get extra credit points for spending more time in reflection and prayer as opposed to tending other life duties and responsibilities. That kind of thinking reflects the old dualism that has long infested Christianity, which pits the love of God and love of neighbour against one another.

So will this hermitage time fade? In answer to this question, I have had an experiment happily foisted upon me. Friends from overseas have been with us for four weeks. I spent time with them, and we went on holidays together, and we had a good time. During their visit, I sought to bring the hermitage with me—or, in other words, to internalise my hermitage experience. So how did all that go?

The short answer: with difficulty. Taking time out has clear advantages in terms of a reflective focus. To be with others calls us to be attentive to matters at hand while at the same time seeking to maintain an inner attentiveness and prayerfulness. It can be done, but it is clearly something I need to grow into.

All of this raises some interesting questions regarding the shape of this inner attentiveness. While it involves mental prayer and thoughtful listening, it also involves a movement of prayer that is well beyond rationality. Some call this the prayer of the heart or contemplative prayer. But there can also be an inner longing and groaning that is well beyond words. This form of prayer is more directly influenced by the mysterious Spirit. This is not so much a prayer of enlightenment, but prayer shrouded in the darkness of unknowability, a childlike form of prayer that may well include speaking in tongues. In this form of prayer, we pray with our very being.

Whatever form and shape prayer takes, our first concern is not to press God for the things we think we need or the matters we are concerned about, but rather a quest for God's presence and relationship. Older theology spoke of the beautific vision of God. In this quest, one thing is clear: we wait. God reveals himself/herself in peculiar ways and seemingly never at our beck and call. Waiting is thus a key posture of faith—and we often wait for what we may never fully receive or understand.

To pray with our being is a form of birthing prayer. We see with the eyes of faith what is not, or what is distorted, or what could be enhanced, and we yearn to see these things rectified. In this way of praying, we humbly offer ourselves to the birthing Spirit, who wishes to use our longings and prayers in this renewing process. Here, of course, we stumble into what seems most preposterous. For the sovereign Spirit surely does not need us and can well work apart from us. But the Spirit, while sovereign, also dwells within us in some mysterious way. The Spirit is both universal and also particular and personal. Hence some synchronicity is possible. How awesome! What an invitation! How mysterious!

8

Attentiveness

24 July 2016

I began this journey on April 1, and I am a little shocked that it is already the end of July. I never thought that time could go so quickly when I'm not doing anything much at all. In preparing for this sabbatical, I thought this time would drag.

When we step out from under the tyranny of time amidst our busy activities of life, we experience a different sense of time. In our normal circumstances, time is a hard task-master. Sabbatical time is a gift—a playful and renewing time. During our normal routines and schedules, time is an "enemy," but during Sabbath, time is a friend. I am deeply grateful for this gift of time.

I do get questions from some of my friends regarding my expected outcomes for this sabbatical. And some want to know whether anything special has happened by way of insight and revelation. To the first question, the answer is simple enough: I felt called to let my life lie, like a fallow field, for an extended period of time. Regarding the second question, I have not had great flashes of light and insight. But I trust that something has been taking place within me, which in time will become apparent by the way I live and the choices that I make.

But I think there is a "sleeper" question here as well. Is Sabbath time or time for meditation and reflection all about me or someone else? We Westerners, in particular, tend to assume that it is all about me, in the sense of making me a "better" person—more prayerful and more caring.

But perhaps Sabbath time is primarily about God. Instead of attending to my issues and my world, what about attending to God? What about giving God my time and attention even when there are no flashes of enlightenment?

Right now, this orientation is most meaningful to me. In our contemporary world, where God is so neglected, I think we need to honour God with our love through attentiveness. This is my probing journey at this time—and who knows what may be its fruit?

9

Crying Out

1 August 2016

In an earlier reflection, I touched on the matter of prayer. Let me share a few more thoughts about this challenging topic—challenging because I believe that prayer has become a crisis issue in the contemporary church.

First, the problem is not with understanding prayer as an intimate language with God, where we cry "Abba Father." Nor is the problem with holding prayer as a deep and longing sigh beyond words. And most moderns are familiar and comfortable with prayer as a contemplative experience.

But the problem comes when we pray for something or someone, specifically asking God to grant our request. Many questions swirl around this form of prayer. Am I forcing God's hand? Is it God's will? Am I asking this in faith? What are my motives? Has God got other and more pressing things to tend? Do I know what is best in making this request? The questions go on and on, and they can immobilise us.

Let me be more specific. I began this hermitage journey in the beginning of April. The hermitage is set in open forest and is surrounded by a lot of landscaping, including young trees and flowering plants. As weeks went by without any rain, I felt the lament of nature and its cry for rain. I was also deeply aware of the longstanding drought in much of Queensland and the suicide of farmers who had been giving in to despair. So I began to pray for rain—not my only specific prayer request, but a focus nonetheless.

And rain came, and it has come since. And with three major rain events over the past couple of months, much of drought-stricken Queensland has had significant rainfalls. The bush around the hermitage is smiling!

So I should be smiling too! While I am thankful, I have been left with many questions. These, I think, form something of the crisis of prayer. Among these questions are the following: did my prayers have anything to do with the coming of rain? Maybe, maybe not? Surely, many others have been praying much more fervently for rain than me! Did God specifically send the rain, or has God given the forces of nature a certain autonomy? In other words, is every event of nature a God event? I am not sure. When there is no rain, is God displeased? When it rains, is God being generous? I am not so sure about this either. It sounds too simplistic.

These considerations raise other questions. What is the ongoing relationship between God and the created order? What is the relationship between God and humanity? Does God do what we ask? Does God do only what God chooses to do in God's wisdom and sovereignty? And what is our responsibility in all of this? Do we also affect nature? If we took better care of the earth, would rain be more prevalent?

These questions—and these are by no means exhaustive—are real and tiring. So do we give up on prayer because we can't find satisfactory answers to these questions? Or do we pray anyway, in the face of mystery, where some prayers come about while others do not? In Scripture, the call to pray is clear enough. Answers to prayer are out of our hands. So maybe it is all about trusting the God who both gives and withholds.

Maybe prayer is a child's cry in the face of our great needs and so many things that we cannot do. In Christian prayer, this cry is directed to the God whose face we most clearly see in Jesus Christ. To cry out is already a comfort.

10

Seeing

4 August 2016

Many Christians think that living a monastic life is a form of escapism, but this is a serious misunderstanding. Monks live in community for the glory of God, a life of prayer, the practice of hospitality, and they are involved in various forms of service. In the Benedictine monasteries I have visited, their service was focused on conducting secondary schools. In Franciscan communities, their focus was to serve the poor.

Whether we are in a monastery, a hermitage, or practicing prayer and meditation at home, work, or in a recreational space, we should never seek to escape the realities of our world. In fact, we withdraw in order to be with God in friendship and love and to see our world more clearly so that we can engage it from a more prayerful space.

In my hermitage journey, there have been days when the pain and injustice of our world have been so present that I have felt overwhelmed and despairing. The issues for me have not only been the arenas of armed conflict and the acts of terrorism—tragic as these are—but also the global moves towards various forms of dictatorship, the erosion of values of care in many of our institutions, the mistreatment of minorities, the blatant promotion of fear in our societies, the increasing fragility of those in the job market, and the incessant celebration of economic rationalism and pragmatism. As individuals we have become little play balls in our societies—easily deflated and assigned to the scrap heap.

Jesus' promise, "fear not, little flock, for it is your Father's good pleasure to give you the kingdom" (Luke 12: 32), seems so remote, and this increases my sense of despair. Now, of course, I am aware of the New Testament theological concept of the "yet" and "not yet" nature of the Kingdom of God and that we are to continue to pray for the kingdom's coming (Matthew 6: 10). I realise that we are but pilgrims here, and the fullness of the kingdom awaits us in God's eschatological future. But I am longing to see more signs of the kingdom—not for the sake of the spectacular, but for the greater healing of humanity.

Yet the gift of the kingdom that Luke refers to is the presence of God the king in the face of Jesus Christ, the suffering servant. This presence is communal, for the gift continues in the presence of the Spirit dwelling in the faith community that seeks to live in the way of Jesus. This way of life is contrary to the kingdoms of this world, for it takes part in sacrificial service so that God's restorative and healing presence may percolate more fully in our world.

Three key signs of the kingdom of God are restored community in Christ, intercession for our world, and a service in the world that seeks God's shalom and justice. If these marks are God's gift and challenge to us who, two thousand years later, stand in the tradition of Jesus' promise to his little flock, then our sense of despair and indifference will need to be transformed into a living hope. This hope seeks to fly in the face of all that we see now by seeing what God will yet do in our time. May we have eyes "to see."

11

Seeing Anew

12 August 2016

In these hermitage notes I have made various references to the contemplative experience, which at its heart is being attentive to God. This is basic, and hence the emphasis on the practices of solitude, listening, meditation, and so on.

But one can also say this slightly differently with important consequences. The contemplative experience is being attentive to the *attentive* God. This moves the centre from what we are doing in relation to God to what God is doing in relation to us. The underlying question is not: how can I seek God? But rather: in what ways is God seeking me? And in what ways is God already present and active?

This is an exhilarating question, because it places God at the centre and acknowledges my self-preoccupation, blindness, and lack of faith. More importantly, it invites me to see anew by throwing the net of my gaze as widely as possible. When I am attentive to the attentive God, I ask questions such as: How is God's attentiveness expressed in the daily provisions of my life? in the consolations within my inner being? in my appreciation of nature? in my friendships? in the worship and service of the faith community? in my work-a-day world?

As I ask these questions, my earlier perceptions about God's active presence in the world may change. For if God is attentive and present in my daily work, then God is not *only* active when I, or someone else, receives a vision or healing. For while God may well be in the more spectacular, God is also wonderfully present in the ordinary. And if God is attentive and present in the challenge of a secular colleague, then God is not *only* present in word and sacraments. More profoundly, if God is the very ground of my being, then God is attentive and present in the general movements of history.

Thus the contemplative experience is not about a narrow piety, but rather a wide gaze that takes in all of life. In the language of Ignatian spirituality, we see God in all things.

In our deeply secular and idolatrous Western world, where our gaze is often pulled away from the vision of God, the experience of contemplation needs to grow and deepen within us. This may well save us from despair, renew our faith, and empower us for a more sustained missional presence in the world. Put most simply: activism is the daughter of mysticism.

1 2

Sabbath Space

24 August 2016

This hermitage time has drawn me to reflect on the spirituality of place. We know that spirituality has to do with an inner disposition and orientation, with certain prayer and reflective practices, and with the overall gestalt of one's life and service. We also know that spirituality within the Christian context is part of a particular tradition, be it Reformed, Anabaptist, Benedictine, Ignatian, or Franciscan, among many others.

But does spirituality have anything to do with place? Do monasteries, temples, cathedrals, retreat houses, and other sacred sites enshrine a certain spiritual presence? When we inhabit these places, are we stirred to worship, prayer, and reflection?

Some years ago, my wife and I spent some weeks at Schloss Mittersill in Austria, a castle built in the twelfth century and then rebuilt in the sixteenth century. Its chapel powerfully drew us to prayer. So did the Benedictine monastery outside Mission in British Columbia. So did our visit to the island of Lindisfarne in the UK. Though these experiences were true for us, it is also possible for thousands of tourists to visit the great cathedrals of Europe and be touched by the architecture and sculptures, and yet remain unmoved in their sense of the divine.

But can ordinary places in our homes or offices at work, where we regularly spend time for reflection and prayer, also become "sacred" places inhabited by the brooding presence of the Spirit? Do prayers and cries over years and centuries seep into the walls of ancient chapels? In Celtic spirituality, any place over time can become a "thin place." What is significant is that we engage these places in a certain way—not simply in terms of routine, but rather with a prayerful attentiveness. This may be what we mean when we speak of a peaceful place or home.

As soon as I enter the hermitage, a place that has been set apart for contemplation, I feel drawn to be quiet, reflective, attentive, and prayerful. Maybe we need more of these places in our busy lives and world. Most of our places are geared for productivity and achievement, while there are few places for Sabbath.

1 3

Troubling God

30 August 2016

Besides growing up in a Christian family steeped in the Reformed faith, two other settings shaped my Christian journey: the Charismatic renewal in Brisbane during the 1960s and the so-called Jesus movement of the early 1970s.

Within these three formative realities, I was more or less caught up in something much bigger than myself. This had nothing to do with spiritual self-effort, but rather with being carried along by the movement of the Spirit in these particularly heartwarming and life-giving settings.

Apart from a general sense of being carried along by my participation in the life and faith of the church, I have had little subsequent sense of being caught up by the breath of the Spirit. For me, the Christian life has been much more a journey of plugging along. My months in this hermitage time have reinforced this, for my "plugging along" has often had the flavour of "the dark night" of the soul. Rather than being caught up in something larger than myself, my journey has been a lonely walk of faith.

As I have pondered my journey during this time, I have only come away with more questions. Is our secular Western lifestyle so pervasive that it shapes the tone of our lives? Are we so caught up in secularity that our Christian way of life is but a weak protest, or maybe an even weaker whimper? Is our participation in the life of the church so minimal that it no longer forms or sustains us? Are we, at best, spiritual pilgrims or religious refugees? Most significantly, should we no longer expect a "movement" of the Spirit in our world?

If our lack of prayer and expectation is any indication, then our honest answer would have to be, "yes." This raises a very troubling question: is God simply giving us what we have resigned ourselves to? It may well be so!

But maybe the time has come for Christians, particularly those in the West, to become "God botherers." By this I mean that we need to "trouble" God. Along with the Psalmist, we need to exclaim: "Why, O Lord, do you stand afar off? Why do you hide yourself" (Psalm 10:1). We need to confess: "Arise, O Lord; O God lift up your hand; forget not the afflicted" (Psalm 10:12).

But will we trouble God? Will we tell God that we are desolate? Will we cry out to God to show himself/herself in more significant ways? Will we tell God that we are bereft, that our world is devoid of God's presence and power? Will we ask God to arise, stretch out a healing hand, and bring renewal and peace to our world?

We had better do this. It would be better to trouble God than to neglect and ignore God, thereby neglecting ourselves and our world. For in neglecting God we not only fall into the chaos of isolation, but we will have to bear the burden of our own idolatry.

14

Responding

5 September 2016

The Christian life is framed and sustained by some broad realities. One such framework is the kaleidoscopic biblical narrative rich in its panoramas of God's redemptive and healing action in our world which gives us hope and direction. Another is the diverse reality of the universal church in history, where we can see both the unity and rich diversity of the people of God seeking to be the faithful servants of Christ. A third is the providential nature of God's concern for the whole human race, including those in the faith community. Fourthly, we are all—including those who are not part of the faith community—subject in various ways to the ever-brooding and ever-creative Spirit of God.

But sometimes the Christian life is also characterised by a scary particularity. This particularity has its roots in the Old Testament and is carried into the New Testament. Moses is singled out and called to confront Pharaoh and to "bring my people...out of Egypt" (Exodus 3:10). Jeremiah is called to be "a prophet to the nations" (Jeremiah 1:5). Paul is called to be an apostle "through a revelation of Jesus Christ" (Galatians 1:12).

What about those of us who do not see ourselves as either a leader, prophet, or apostle? Are we also marked by some particularity? Astonishingly, the answer is, "yes"! The Spirit speaks to us today and gives us both a gift and a task. Embrace and calling are the initial movements of the life-giving Spirit.

Rather than embracing the Western Enlightenment notion that freedom constitutes the fundamental nature of what it means to be human, I believe that responding to our calling most significantly indicates who we are. The gestalt of this is a fascinating mosaic. Calling suggests a God who is not only "there," but also seeks to draw us into his/her purposes.

Yet the call of God, whether all-encompassing or marginally significant, always beckons our response. Thus our freedom lies in giving God his/her rightful place in our lives. Responding to this call gives our life its fundamental purpose while also invigorating and forming us. To be fully human is to live God's call with love and purpose.

My hermitage time has been a time of affirmation and struggle. But it has also brought a renewed call to my life. That specific call will become even more obvious in time. But a call is not only challenging and sometimes hard to accept, it is also invigorating. A call is, first and foremost, a grace and blessing rather than a task and duty. A call is not made by us, but initiated by God. This rightly defines who God is as Lord of our lives, and who we are as those who gladly hear and obey.

15

Repentance

14 September 2016

Christian spirituality often highlights the three-dimensional nature of our journey: upward, inward, and outward. Many writers emphasize the intimate relationship between truer self-knowledge and the knowledge of God.

In various other religious spiritualities, there is a strong emphasis on self-knowledge and the stripping away of one's social self in order to find one's inner core or one's enlightened self.

During this hermitage time, although I have embarked on this three-fold journey, I have not found an inner enlightened self. I have found something quite different. Let me try to explain.

We are all shaped by our culture, which defines not only our social self, but also our positional self or status. Thus we tell others that we are an artist, business person, farmer, priest, writer, and so on. Our work-a-day world and our vocation shape us—so much so that some people become their profession, and this role is what others value about them.

Within one's professional status, however, there are deeper contours. I am not just a priest, but an ambitious or conservative priest. I am not just a business person, but one who takes risks. I can either become generous or greedy in the way I live my life. Here we touch on both our orientation as well as our values and ethics. We don't just have a job, for we are motivated by how we function within that job.

Yet our inner quest should go much deeper than these considerations. I may be driven by deep wounding, fears, or insecurities. Or I may be driven by the need to impress, possess, or control.

In pressing further along this inward journey, there is only one domain, and it is not peaceful enlightenment. Rather, it is the arena of confession and seeking the grace of God. We see this pattern in Psalm 51: "Behold, I was brought forth in iniquity" (v. 5); "Create in me a clean heart, O God, and renew a right spirit within me" (v. 10); though "you delight in truth in my inward being...purge me with hyssop, and I shall be clean" (vv. 6, 7); "Have mercy on me, O God, according to your steadfast love; according to your abundant mercy" (v. 1).

On the inner journey we do not just stumble into a cave of light, where all is unsullied and pure. Instead, the inner journey leads us to a deeper repentance, a thirst for the grace and mercy of God. This journey brings us into the embrace of the Other rather than self-enhancement, towards forgiveness rather than self-purity, towards grace rather than self-effort.

16

Hidden Water

19 September 2016

My hermitage time has temporarily shifted from Brisbane to the heart of Australia's red centre. I am on a spiritual retreat in the desert outside of Alice Springs. This one-week retreat run by a Roman Catholic lay couple has focussed on how the desert landscape carries important images and metaphors for the spiritual journey.

In this reflection I wish to focus on the theme of water. In all the time that we spent in the desert—except for a brief thunderstorm—we never saw any water. Yet there were hidden rivers and creeks sustaining not only majestic Red River Gum trees, but Indigenous communities for thousands of years. Thus there was water everywhere, yet nowhere to be seen. Some of the early Western explorers died from thirst in this brutal landscape while literally sitting on top of water. They just did not know where to dig.

The Todd River, which runs through Alice Springs, is called affectionately the "upside-down river." All one sees is sand. Yet dig down far enough, and there are streams of water.

I found this to be a most helpful image. The Christian landscape in the West, including Australia, can be likened to a desert. Christianity is looking pretty bleak. And many churches are merely in survival mode. They are hardly springs of life-giving water. It should not surprise us that many, over the past decades, have vacated the church and begun to look elsewhere—or nowhere at all.

But could the church be likened to the Todd River? Is there water in the church's bleak landscape? I believe there is—but we will have to dig if we are going to drink from it.

If we begin to dig, what will we find? On the surface, we might observe that Christian churches continue to provide many of the social welfare services in the general community. If we dig a little deeper, we may discover Christians within the society who are running ethical enterprises and businesses. If we dig even further, we may discover Christians forming networks of care and practical support.

But we need to dig even deeper, where there are Christians drinking from the deeper wells of Benedictine, Franciscan, Celtic, and Ignatian spirituality. In these hidden "upside down rivers," we will find Christians at prayer for the redemption and humanization of our world and Christians engaged in the quest for peace and justice.

Just as the New Testament calls the faith community to be leaven in a loaf of bread, which like the Todd River cannot be seen, so Christians today are living as a hidden presence in our world. Perhaps this is a good thing. The church no longer holds great social power and influence, as in its Christendom days, but is becoming a "little flock" hidden in the heart of the world.

If these are in anyway appropriate images and metaphors, then everyone will need to dig. Christians will need to dig beyond the crust of a formulaic religion to find the water of life-giving theologies and spiritualities. Seekers will need to dig beyond the media's tired typification of Christianity to find nourishment for anorexic souls that have been brutalised by toxic neo-liberal ideologies and economic practices.

So the word from the desert of central Australia is most basic. There is more to a desert landscape than the desert. There is life-giving water. But one has to dig.

17

Memory and Hope

20 September 2016

One can't be too long on a hermitage journey of quiet reflection before one meets two "friends"—nostalgia and regret. You may be surprised that I regard these as friends, but bear with me.

Nostalgia is a wistful longing for something good from the past. Regret is sadness regarding failure in the past. Both are embedded in memory. At its best, memory engages our present while re-appropriating past events with a view towards future outworking. In memory, the past, present, and future operate together.

Nostalgia, of course, always runs the danger of making some aspect of the past more than it was. This is a distortion. But the word "nostalgia," which comes from the Greek *nostos,* can simply mean homecoming. Thus it is a return to what once was, what now no longer is, what we have lost. If what was lost was true, good, and beautiful, then nostalgia is a friend that re-awakens longings and hope for this to be recovered in the present and in the future. The contemplative experience can awaken these possibilities.

Regret touches our failings and what could have been, where we failed to seize the day and make the most of the opportunities that came our way. Lost opportunities are part of our innerscape, which we are invited to grieve. But we may also use our regrets in service of the future. Doors or windows may open again. A different, but related, pathway may open before us.

Note that I use the phrase "may open up." This is not a mad scramble to make up for the past. We need to release the past and let it rest in the grace of God. But in faith, we can become open to what God may yet do.

Our two "friends" should be welcomed. They may, indeed, be signposts pointing to what is yet to come. And importantly, we should be attentive in the contemplative time, not only to scripture, but also to the movements in our inner being. The feelings that come our way are not to be pushed away as unwelcome intruders. They should be welcomed as special guests.

18

Encountering

26 September 2016

During the Alice Springs' retreat, a surprising phrase—"the gaze of Christ"—was repeated a number of times. To twenty-first century urbanites, this phrase may sound overly speculative or emotional. For no one has time to gaze at us—let alone God. Despite our technological connectedness, we often feel isolated. Spiritually, we feel more like orphans than God's beloved sons and daughters.

In John's Gospel, the phrase "gaze of Christ" is used when Jesus interacts with the Samaritan woman (chapter 4). This chapter speaks about Jesus' close encounter with this woman, where he gazes so deeply into her life that the woman later exclaims to the people of her town: "he told me everything I ever did" (John 4:39).

In reflecting on this encounter, I was struck by its depiction of two kinds of gazing: the direct gaze and the deflected gaze—or the direct and indirect encounter. The direct encounter takes place between Jesus and this woman at the well. The indirect encounter occurs when the woman returns to her home, tells her neighbours about her interaction with Jesus, and "many Samaritans from that town believed in him because of the woman's testimony" (John 6:39).

The continuation of Christianity in our world most often occurs through the deflected gaze or the indirect encounter. Thus people come to faith in Christ through the witness of others. And it is well and good for us to point one another in the right direction, along a saving pathway.

But in the West, where the life of faith is so readily battered and undermined, I wonder if the indirect encounter is enough anymore. Perhaps if faith in this world is going to continue and grow, it will need to be spawned by a direct encounter, a direct gaze. To put that in somewhat different language, faith entered into because of others—particularly family and friends—or at an emotional moment in a church setting can hardly endure the constant undermining of our critical and cynical culture. Thus only a direct mystical encounter with Christ, rather than a mediated Christ, can sustain us.

This theme also occurs in John's narrative. When the Samaritans urge Jesus to come and stay with them, the townsfolk encounter Christ directly and say to the Samaritan woman: "We no longer believe just because of what you said; now we have heard for ourselves, and we know that this man really is the Saviour of the world" (John 4:42).

If the Christian faith is going to survive in our world, particularly in the West, we must hope that our mediated encounters with Christianity will be transformed into direct encounters with Christ through the life-giving Spirit.

19

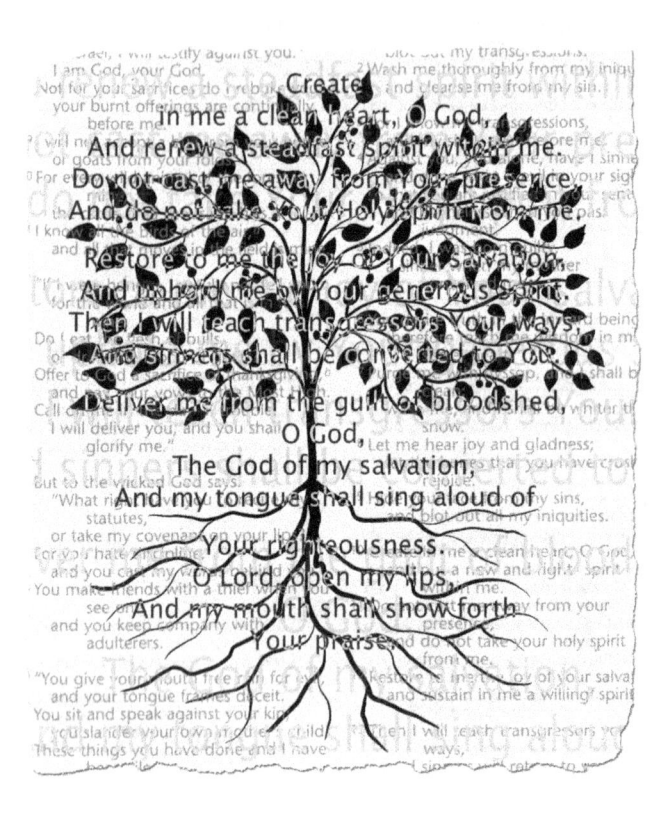

For the Life of the World

28 September 2016

Older theologies of the Christian church emphasised reading the "two books of God"— with the first book being Scripture and the second book being nature, which was seen as a partial revelation of God.

In our modern world we seem to have forgotten this second book. The world has become disenchanted, no longer seen as God's creation, but *only* as the product of a complexity of natural forces.

I have a deep love of nature, which speaks to me about the beauty of God. And sometimes nature speaks to me more directly, as it did during the Alice Springs retreat. Early one morning, while I was gazing at the West

MacDonnell Ranges, dark, swift clouds rolled toward the southeast. Then a lower band of lighter clouds began to skim northwest along the top of the ranges. This double movement went on for quite some time.

The dominant upper clouds brought to my mind the powerful factors of our global world, while the lower wispy clouds seemed to represent the faith community. These shifting clouds reminded me that our faith community, though similar to the broader community, needs to be moving in the opposite direction. We need to be moving towards the love of God, rather than the exultation of humanity; towards forgiveness, rather than hatred; towards community, rather than individualism; towards peacemaking, rather than war-mongering; towards caring for others, rather than self-interest; towards living in the way of Jesus, rather than religiosity; towards being led by the Spirit, rather than dwelling on our own accomplishments.

While the church often exists as a conformist institution in our world, it needs to become more of a counter-community—not one that isolates itself and becomes self-absorbed, but rather a community that offers itself for the life of the world. Such a community will be incarnational and will sow the seeds of goodness and shalom in our world.

Is such a thing possible? Yes! But only if the faith community finds its true identity in the gestalt of Christ through the birthing Spirit. And importantly, are we willing to walk the challenging, and sometimes suffering, road of being a prophetic community in the wider culture, rather than simply being a maintenance institution?

20

A Long Journey

29 September 2016

My six-month hermitage journey is coming to an end at the New Norcia Benedictine Monastery in Western Australia. After a few days here, I will visit some of the Indigenous communities where we used to work in the late 1950s and early 1960s, and then I will be on my way to Manila to teach. I expect that much of my life will be back to normal.

    Benedictine Monasteries carry a special message. The sung liturgies that punctuate their days remind us of the beauty of the Psalms and the importance of praise and worship. The monks remind us that we, too, need to stop in our day for moments of attentiveness, reflection, prayer, and thanksgiving.

Their rhythms of worship, work, and study challenge us to live more integrated, re-collected lives. So often we live with all work and no play, activity with little reflection, externalisation without attending to our inner life. As a consequence, our lives are lopsided and off-centre, which often causes us to be reactionary, fickle, quick to act, and slow in perseverance.

This wonderful spiritual tradition also teaches us a spirituality of the ordinary, where we learn to see the Spirit already at work in our daily lives rather than waiting for something spectacular.

The Benedictines also teach us the spirituality of stability. We so readily rush from one thing to another rather than learning to hang in for the long haul.

Finally, in addition to the gift of welcome and hospitality, Benedictine monks remind us to embrace a "conversion of life." Simply put, our conversions are only small steps in following Christ. More conversions are called for. The journey continues. We have a long way to go.

These days in New Norcia amidst the beauty of an Australian spring are a sign of both hope and challenge. My hope is that we all may drink more deeply at the wells God has provided. My challenge will be to carry the monastery and the hermitage back into my regular daily life.

The Journey Home

1

The Call to Return

20 November 2016

From the first of April through the end of September, I "downed" tools by withdrawing from all my normal activities in order to spend time in a hermitage listening, reflecting, and praying. I am deeply grateful for this time, even though no great revelations came my way, and the time in many ways was quite ordinary. But it may well be more significant than what I realize at present.

    Since this time has refreshed me and has reaffirmed that I continue in much of what I was engaged in previously (but hopefully in new ways), I have returned to these activities, which include teaching, writing, various forms of mission, and the work of protest in the face of the injustices that continue to pervade our world.

But the notion of "return" has captured my imagination, and this is the journey I must now make. This is not a theme that is strong in our contemporary culture. In fact, the opposite is the case, for we are endlessly making decisions and putting strategies in place in order to move forward.

So often we want to move on, move forward, even when careful reflection and looking back might better serve us. As individuals, we are quite happy to move on from one broken relationship to another without thinking about gaining self-insight or entertaining the possibility of reconciliation. And as a contemporary culture, we seem to be quite enamoured with moving ever closer towards right-wing fascism without learning from past atrocities.

So in the coming months, I hope to explore a very basic philosophy, psychology, theology, and practice of "the return." I am somewhat apprehensive about this invitation.

For when we return to a place where we once lived, we are often disturbed and even disappointed because the place has changed, and we have changed as well. There is a dissonance and a sense of disconnect. We also wonder whether our memory is playing tricks on us.

The call to return is writ large in the pages of Scripture. Jacob, after his long sojourn with his uncle Laban in the land of Paddan-aram (Genesis 28:1–5), hears Yahweh's call: "Return to the land of your ancestors and to your kindred" (Genesis 31:3). Jeremiah proclaims: "Return, faithless Israel, says the Lord. I will not look on you in anger, for I am merciful" (Jeremiah 3:12). And the healed demoniac is told by Jesus: "Return to your home, and declare how much God has done for you" (Luke 8:39).

None of these returns are, in and of themselves, easy and straightforward. If we were to follow the healed man back to his town or village, we can readily sense the unease: *what will I say? will the townspeople understand? how will I settle back?* And possibly, beneath all these: *why should I go back to the place that banished me in the first place?* And further: *I really want to be with Jesus. I don't want to go back to this dreary community.*

But the call to return is there. I, too, must make this journey.

2

Returning as a Pilgrim

28 November 2016

Implicit in the notion of "the return" is that one has moved away to another place for some time. This move away can become the material for many a varied story. In our contemporary culture, this move is often made without careful reflection. After all, the world has become our backyard, and we see ourselves as the nomads of the global village.

However, while it is one thing to sightsee the world, it is quite another thing to move away from place, relationships, and work as a reaction to an orchestrated unhappiness and dissatisfaction. In this sense, the move away is framed by the hope that happiness will readily be found elsewhere. This hope can easily falter on the shoals of further disappointments. Thus some sort of return may well be necessary to break this unhappy cycle.

Tragically, there are many in our conflicted and unjust world who move because life is no longer durable in the face of famine, rising sea levels, armed conflict, and many forms of discrimination. Over sixty million such people are presently on the move. For these nomads there may never be a return—and for many, there is no place of real welcome either.

Economic necessity causes others to move. Millions in the Majority World are working overseas to help their families back home gain a better future while enduring the pain of being separated from spouses, parents and siblings.

The biblical narratives are replete with these themes. Many people move because of famines (Genesis 47:20; 2 Kings 6:25; Jeremiah 24:10), which are sometimes framed by God's judgment on his people. More prominently, many are called by God to go elsewhere in order to fulfill God's purposes, beginning with Abraham (Genesis 12:1) and continuing on to the call for the early church to bring the gospel to the nations (Matthew 28:19–20). In the church's long march in history, many have heard and responded to such a call.

My wife and I made such moves a number of times, and none of them has (or have) been easy. But along with the loss of leaving loved ones, we have also received the gift of learning from other cultures and gaining new friends.

The big shock, however, has been our return. Because we cannot repair the loss of years away, homecomings are almost always conflicted. We are no longer at "home" in our former familiar place. And we do not live between two or more cultures, but rather in both. We are neither fully away, nor fully home.

In the pain of this tension, there is a strange blessing, a nudge that helps us to realise the fundamental sojourner status of our human existence. Life moves towards death. And for the Christian, there is the sense that this world as it is now is not our final home. Having made the return, our pilgrim status in the journey of faith becomes even more evident. This reminds us that in some strange way we are too early for heaven and too late for this world.

3

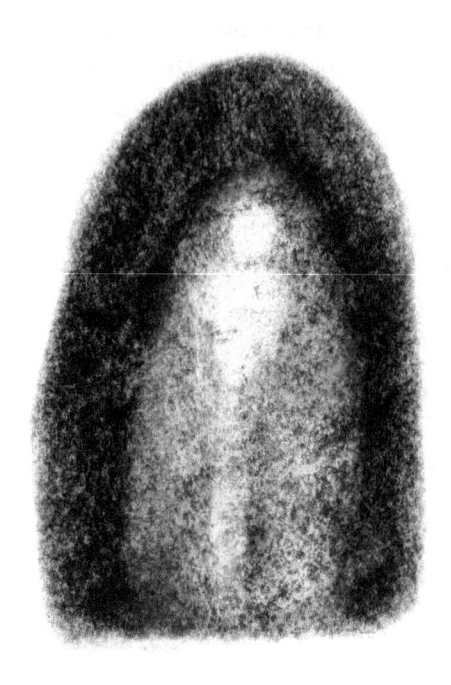

Returning as Stranger

5 December 2016

The notion of "the return" not only holds the many factors that caused us to move away in the first place, but also our condition upon our return. The hope is that we come back in better shape, having gained something that we can bring back to our family and community.

Several biblical narratives carry these archetypal themes, particularly the story of Moses, whose *move away* is cast in the darkest of circumstances, and whose *return* is marked by redemption with the colours of struggle.

Moses, an Israelite outsider within Egyptian culture, becomes a man of privilege and status when adopted into Pharaoh's household (Exodus 2:1–10). He regains his outsider status when he intentionally kills an Egyptian "bully" (2:12). Then he flees to save his now miserable life. This is hardly a great start in the *move away*. Stripped of the possibility of redemption, one would assume that this is where the story ends—with Moses as a criminal and fugitive.

Even though Moses finds new life through the hospitality of a stranger in Midian (Exodus 2:15–21), he continues to see himself as "an alien residing in a foreign land" (2:22). Does this mean that he longs for home and wants to return? We have no way of knowing, but we do know that he is afraid to return because he fears for his life. Yahweh assures him: "Go back to Egypt; for those who were seeking your life are dead" (4:19), suggesting that Moses has been away a long time.

Moses did not instigate his return, because of his criminal identity and his fear of retaliation. But in the burning bush, Moses encounters the redemptive God and receives a revelatory call: "So come, I will send you to Pharaoh to bring my people, the Israelites, out of Egypt" (Exodus 3:10). Here is a miraculous encounter with the "I am who I am" (3:14), who prevails over all of Moses' excuses (3:13–15; 4:1; 4:10), turns a criminal fugitive into a leader with a God-given liberation mandate to break the power of oppression and lead Yahweh's people into the land of freedom.

One can hardly script a more foundational story. The villain becomes the hero. The fugitive becomes the liberator.

The psychology of this story suggests that the demeaned escapee becomes a new self, transformed in the purgation of time, the desert, and the call of God. And in this new fullness, he makes "the return."

My wife, Rita, and I have made a number of returns: we returned from working with Indigenous communities in Western Australia; we returned from working in the Philippines; many years later we returned from Canada to Australia. Most recently, I returned from my time at the hermitage to normal life.

Did we come back as a fuller self? Did we come back at God's call? Did we come back with a grand mission? The answer to the last question, is, "no." The answer to the middle question, is, "we believe so." The answer to the first question, is, "we don't know." What we do know is that no one back home has cared too much. Moses was also plagued by the idea that no one would listen to him (Exodus 4:1). Maybe, in the return, one has become too much a stranger?

4

Returning with Glory

16 December 2016

The six months of downtime at the hermitage was peaceful and reflective. I somehow felt cocooned. I am quite sure that people were praying for me. During that whole period, nothing untoward happened. There were no crises or difficulties. Looking back, this now seems like a miracle.

My return, however, has been exactly the opposite. In coming back to normal life, I have experienced many difficulties within a matter of weeks: exposure to the extra-judicial drug killing issues in Manila, a car breakdown, a family death, a close friend diagnosed with cancer in Brisbane, a family member's job loss in Sydney, along with personal health issues. Coming one after the other, my sense has been that these difficulties are under marching orders.

We can interpret such an onset of difficulties in many different ways. Secularity says this is just circumstantial. The hyper-Christian might suggest that this is God's punishment for some reason. But we can also identify a pattern in our unfolding narratives based on what we see outlined in Scripture and then repeated in Christian biography.

While we do need to be careful that we don't over-correlate what happens in our lives with events in the biblical narratives, as Christians we are invited to make sense of our lives in the light of Scripture. It is also possible that some normativity is at play. By this I mean that our relationship with Christ should be of such a nature that his life is "repeated" in us.

This leads me to the transfiguration event as recorded in the Gospels, which is followed by Jesus' encounter with a boy in distress due to the work of the Evil One (Mark 9:2–29). There is something paradigmatic in this story. Peter, James, and John witness a heavenly event and have a visionary experience that is so marvellous that Peter seems to imply that they all should stay on this mountain top (Mark 9:5). But the experience is a temporary one, and they need to make the return down the mountain, where they are immediately faced with difficulty, distress, and someone in deep need. Jesus cures the boy and challenges his disciples to a deeper life of prayer (Mark 9:29).

There is more to this story than the *ying* and *yang* of *life* or, more colloquially, the fact that we all have good days and bad days. Said differently, we can't stay on the mountain top of a grand experience, for we have to come down to the valley of difficulties and get our hands dirty. This may well be one way to think about this narrative. But the deeper challenge of the story is to carry the "glory" of the mountain top into the challenges of daily life. The contemplative experience always pulls us back to the love of neighbour and service in our world. But our pull into the world and its needs, issues and challenges, needs to come from a place where we have encountered the living God. Thus while we come with humility, our hands are not empty and our hearts are not dull. We have seen something of the "glory" of God. Thus we come in faith and hope.

Communion

1

Disorientation

14 January 2017

I can't begin to describe how difficult it has been to return to normal life activities after my six months in the hermitage. Put most simply, I feel both disoriented and lost.

Surprisingly, my disorientation has nothing to do with the fact that my hermitage time was particularly magnificent, insightful, or spiritually uplifting. In almost every way, it was ordinary: to be still, reflective, and prayerful seemed so basic, and I have no sense that I gained any spiritual "brownie points."

My disorientation also has nothing to do with being in anyway unhappy about returning to normal activities. For I am glad to be back into the fray of life with all of its challenges.

But I have not regained a sense about how to live with the hermitage in my heart. I am restless, and I now find it difficult to engage in the spiritual disciplines.

What is clear is that I am more deeply concerned about the shape of our world: the unsustainable neo-liberal way of life and its exploitation of workers, the lack of caring human values and a commitment to the common good, the political failures to make hard decisions regarding the planet, and the dysfunction of so many of our basic institutions. These things trouble me more than ever, and I feel more powerless than ever.

I feel powerless to be even a small catalyst for change. I feel powerless spiritually, because my prayer seems haphazard and my hope battered.

I wonder where any answers may lie. Scripture is there, but in many ways God seems silent. The Spirit may be brooding, but signs of the Spirit's renewing work are meagre.

Yet what is also clear is that resignation is not an option for me. I need to be engaged, but I am having difficulty discerning the nature of my engagement.

Maybe lament is the way to be in the world? Maybe there are other options?

You can see how lost I am.

2

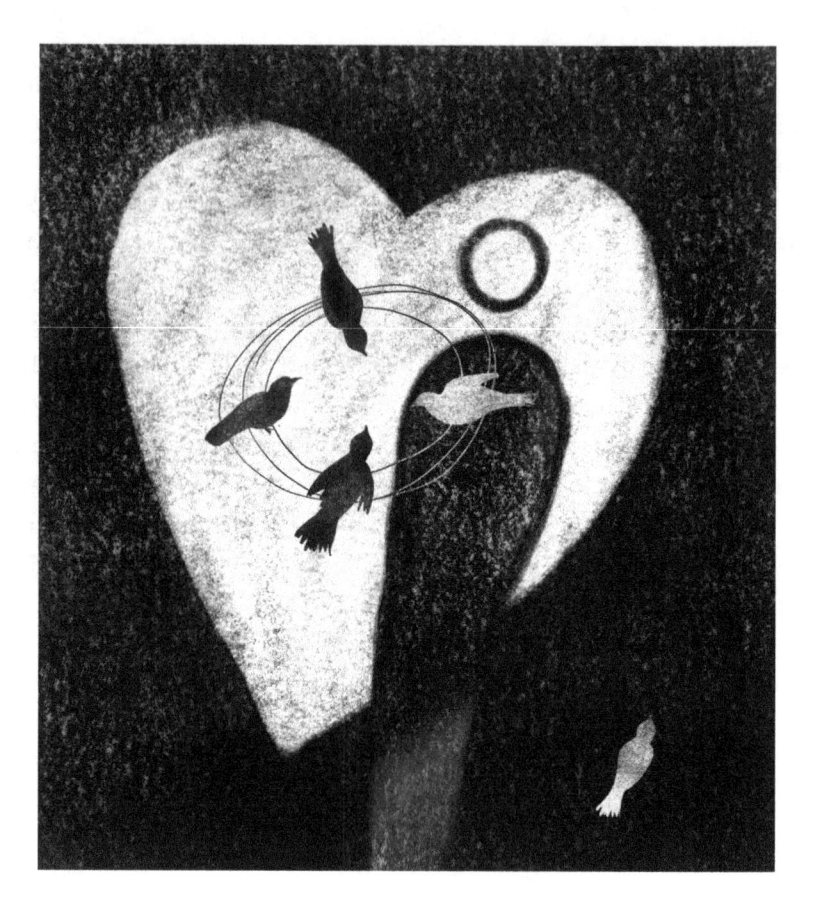

Iminination

14 February 2017

Much of what we experience in daily life is pretty routine. Some is downright boring. Rather than looking down on this, we are invited to live a spirituality of the ordinary. This means that we are thankful for the ordinary, and we hold in our hearts the joy that God is with us in the ordinary.

But we also experience moments and seasons when things are pretty special. In these times, goodness and beauty are "giddy" in their abundance. While my hermitage time was not "giddy," it was special because it was a very different routine and way of life.

Even now, some months later, I am still coming to terms with my time in the hermitage. Along with this, I am wondering if the hermitage journey can reside in my heart amidst a more ordinary rhythm of life.

I think this is possible in two ways. Most basically, my hermitage journey resides within me as a memory. While this can be the fodder for nostalgia, it can also be fertile: a memory that is both pregnant and productive. Such memory draws on the goodness of those months at the hermitage and is productive for the future. Here, a memory in the present looks to the past as a challenge for the future. The challenge is to make the hermitage an internal disposition and discipline.

This brings me to the second possibility. Can I build a hermitage within my inner being? Can this be meaningful? Can I make time to enter there? This is not *place* as a hermitage, but the *heart* as a hermitage. Or better still, this is a hermitage somewhere within the heart, for we carry so many things within our hearts. So much presses in upon us. We are internally busy and often distracted.

This is an old invitation, where in the midst of our busy days, we cross through portals to an inner quiet, an inner solitude, as if entering a hermitage, monastery, or quiet place in nature.

In my imagination, I have crafted the hermitage in my being. I am learning to enter there. This is much more difficult than going to an actual hermitage. I am learning, but have a lot to learn.

3

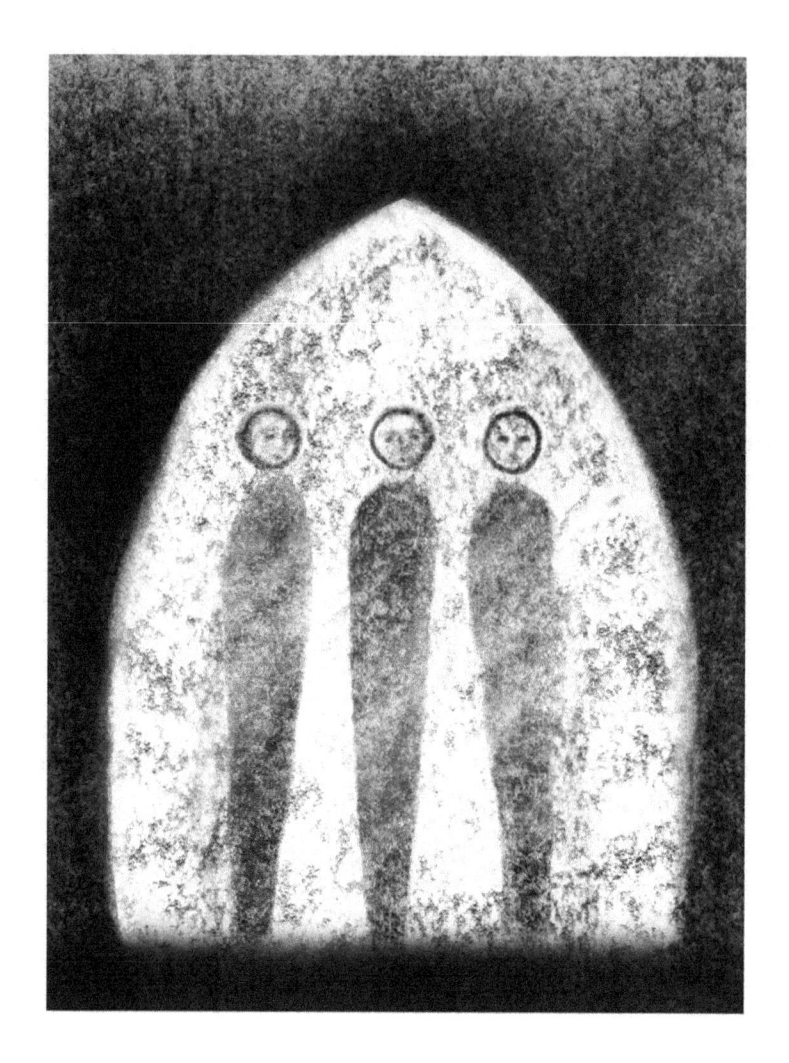

Connection

15 February 2017

The Christian life does not flourish through inner gazing, and it never prospers by keeping a record of our achievements. Nor is it enhanced by constant archaeological expeditions into our inner being or regularly taking the pulse of our spiritual state.

The Christian life comes as gift, the gift of the grace of Christ and the sustaining presence of the Spirit. It is shaped by the ethos of the biblical narrative and sustained by our participation in the faith community. It has to do with "the way" of Christ growing within our lives and outworking itself in the manner through which we seek to bless others. It is lived and sustained by the love and prayers of others and by the great "cloud of witnesses" who have gone before us throughout the ages.

While my time at the hermitage, along with the practice of cultivating a hermitage within my heart, involves withdrawal and solitude, we are never alone. Put simply, we are woven into a web of relationships. Some are visible and obvious, and others are unseen and mystical.

So while we have our networks of family, friends, members of the faith community, and others who think of us and may pray for us, there are also those who are prompted by the Spirit to pray. We often have no idea of those who are supporting us in some spiritual way.

Moreover, our lives are connected with the writers of the biblical narrative, and we are in-dwelt by the writings of Christian authors who encourage us and enrich our lives. They draw us out of the limitations of our self-construction and self-enhancement, enlarging us through growth and transformation. After all, we are not simply solo selves, but selves embedded in community.

But we are also linked to Christ, the faithful Son of the Father, who has, through adoption, brought us into the community of the Trinity. We are not simply "in Christ," but we are also in the Spirit, and therefore in the gaze and love of the Father.

Thus the hermitage in the heart is not simply a lonely place, for there are many links and nodes of connections. We are wired into a network. These wires hum with life.

4

This Day

2 April 2017

In the realm of a lived spirituality, we don't have bank accounts where we can make regular deposits over many months and then simply draw on the surplus. Thus even though I spent a lot of time reflecting and praying in a hermitage for six months, I can't simply coast along now and draw from my credit in the bank. There is no credit.

A lived spirituality is about each day. Just because my time with God was intense last week, my focus is not about what happened then, but rather with what is happening or not happening today.

This, of course, does not mean that we will always live out our spirituality at the same level, for there will be times of intensity and times of levelling off. This is the very nature of relationships.

So my concern is not with the general, but with the specifics of each day. On this day, am I willing to mark out some small periods for solitude? Can I dig a well of stillness? Will I be attentive to the Spirit and to the Spirit's movement within my inner being? Am I open to God's inspiration and desires? Will I be restless, driven, and distracted, or will I listen and be attentive?

While there is such a dynamic as "prevenient grace" (John Wesley), I do make choices regarding what happens in this day. The reality of this choice highlights the reality of my struggle. I can either cooperate or resist. I can be wise or foolish.

May we enter this day well, held in the words of the Gospel: "I do believe; help my unbelief" (Mark 9:24). Each day, may we pray: *Grace my weak desires with the strength of your goodness. Amen.*